CW01018199

__ow
to Pass

Branch Banking —
Law and Practice

How to Pass

Branch Banking — Law and Practice

Geoffrey Sales ACIB

The Chartered Institute of Bankers

First Published 1990
Second Edition, 1992

BANKERS BOOKS LIMITED
c/o The Chartered Institute of Bankers
10 Lombard Street
London EC3V 9AS

CIB publications are published by The Chartered Institute of Bankers, a non-profit making, registered educational charity, and are distributed exclusively by Bankers Books Limited which is a wholly-owned subsidiary of The Chartered Institute of Bankers.

British Library Cataloguing-in-Publication Data

Sales, Geoffrey
    How to Pass Branch Banking: Law and Practice
    2 Rev. ed. (How to Pass Series)
    I. Title II. Series
    332.1

ISBN 0 85297 321 7

Typeset in 10/12pt Times, printed on 80 gsm paper; cover on 240 gsm
Printed by Commercial Colour Press, London

How to Pass
Branch Banking — Law and Practice

Contents

Preface to Second Edition

Since the first edition of this book, the title of the subject has changed and a new chief examiner has been appointed.

The new title, Branch Banking – Law and Practice, is much more descriptive of the content than the old Practice of Banking 1 was. In order to be successful, candidates need a sound grasp of the legal principles in practical situations.

The structure of the examination paper changed in May 1991. The main changes are:

(1) Pass mark 51% not 60%;

(2) Section A — one compulsory question;

(3) Section B — answer two questions from three;

(4) Section C — answer two questions from three;

(5) All questions carry 20 marks;

(6) Candidates must satisfy the examiner in Section B and C of the paper by obtaining a minimum of 16 marks in each section.

In his address to students in the Institute library on 31 March 1992, Walter Hall, chief examiner, said that his questions would tend to be a little more branch-orientated than those of his predecessor. As an example, he said that in securities questions an understanding of the clauses in security forms and the procedures for perfecting securities (as typical branch activities) would receive more frequent attention than the considerations upon liquidation (which in practice tend to be taken out of branch hands).

Preface to First Edition

Anyone who knows me well will tell you that I am not, by nature, a boastful person. I've often been told that I undersell myself and that I must not hide my light under a bushel. What I'm about to say will come as a pleasant surprise to those people:

I AM AN EXPERT AT PASSING EXAMS!

Consider the following evidence. I passed seven out of nine subjects at O level, three out of three at A level, and all five subjects at the first attempt in the Institute's Diploma (there were only five subjects until 1980). Nothing too remarkable about that, I can hear you saying. Doubtless there are many of you out there who can top that — but wait! That's not my claim to fame. It is the manner in which I passed that prompts me to claim expert status.

No, I didn't win any prizes — quite the reverse. At O level the pass mark was 45%, and in each of the seven subjects I passed, I got between 45% and 60%. The pass mark at A level was 40% — I got 45% in two subjects and 60% in the third. In four out of the five Institute Diploma papers I got *exactly* the pass mark.

In other words, I did just enough to scrape through in 15 out of 17 exams — *at the first attempt*! Now come on — admit it! It takes a certain talent to do that. It's exam technique gone mad!

Obviously, the Institute, in their wisdom, thought that I might have something worth passing on to others studying for the Associateship examinations, and in particular Branch Banking — Law and Practice, which I've taught under different titles since 1977. I have also conducted revision courses in the subject for the Institute, both in Lombard Street and overseas.

When writing this guide, I was conscious of the background against which most of you will be studying for this paper. I have assumed that time will be a problem. I know you have to work during the day and study in the evening — I know there are demands on your time at the weekend!

We need to reduce the huge syllabus to a manageable size by prioritising the content. I'll then look at the information sources available to you, consider exam technique and conclude by reviewing methods of revision. But first, why do people fail?

Geoffrey Sales, ACIB

PART 1

Reasons for Failing

Lack of knowledge

Let there be no doubts! Branch Banking — Law and Practice is a knowledge subject. Without detailed knowledge, no amount of exam technique will get you through.

So, put in the hours! Work hard at achieving the necessary level of knowledge in the following areas:

(a) Facts — of the various topics in the syllabus.
(b) Cases — generous marks are available for quoting relevant cases. You only need to identify the case, e.g., *'Tournier case'* is sufficient. You don't need to quote the full title of the case.
(c) Statutes — marks are awarded for identifying relevant statutes, e.g., Cheques Act 1957, s.1.

Your knowledge has to be precise. For example, when a joint account holder dies, any credit balance passes automatically to the survivor. Many students cite the reason for this as being the clause in the joint account mandate which states that fact. This is not so. The real reason is the common law rule of survivorship. The bank cannot rely on the clause in the mandate because death of one party cancels the mandate. The clause is there simply as proof of the intention of the parties, so that if there is any dispute from other parties when the balance is transferred to the survivor, the bank can point to the clause to justify its action.

Lack of thought

You must not rush into answering a question! Stop to think! It doesn't matter how much you know about a topic; if it's the wrong topic, you score no marks.

So, before you start to write, be sure you have recognised what the question is getting at.

Give yourself at least five minutes. During that time, start to map out your answer. Get your facts together and sort them out into some sort of logical order. Having done that, it shouldn't take you long to actually write your answer.

Verbosity

The quality of answers is not judged by the weight of paper used. Open up any examiner's report, and you will see the chief examiner begging for tabulated answers in note form. Essays are not required. Therefore, do not write:

> The bank needs to register the company charge at Companies House within 21 days pursuant to section 395 of the Companies Act 1985, otherwise the charge will be void against a liquidator or administrator and any creditor.

Instead, write:

> Register charge at Comp. House within 21 days — otherwise void against liquidator or administrator and any creditor — Companies Act 1985, s. 395.

Lack of technique

Imagine this as an examination question:

If I were to throw a stone at you, what would you do?

Your answer would be probably short and sweet:

I'd get out of the way.

In the exam, you would miss marks with that answer. Reasons would be required. The answer should read:

Stones hurt — can cause serious injury, even death — I'd get out of the way, and thus avoid injury.

Ironically, practical experience can be a disadvantage because the more familiar you are with the subject matter, the more likely you are to omit from your answers those facts which are second nature to you. You must discipline yourself to state the obvious.

This is where exam technique comes in.

PART 2

Priorities

Let's start by having a look at the winning post. The pass mark is 51. You have to answer FIVE questions, each worth 20 marks.

Section A consists of one *compulsory* question based on any part of the syllabus. Section B deals with a wide range of topics covering banking operations and the banker-customer relationship. Section C dels with fewer individual topics but some of them, for example, land, are so vast that they provide the examiner with plenty of scope for setting questions. You will have to answer two questions from each of Sections B and C.

The syllabus is enormous. So, the first job is to cut it down to size by prioritising the subject-matter. Here are a few facts:

(a) There have been questions on LAND in every exam set since April 1980;

(b) Most past exams have included something on COMPA-NIES;

(c) There have been over 20 questions on some aspect of CHEQUES since April 1980.

Now for a statement of the obvious. You can't omit these three areas from your studies. They must occupy a significant proportion of your time.

After that, you need to do some detective work and to use some common sense. For example, if there was a full question on status enquiries at the last sitting, the chance of a question at this sitting is fairly slim. Let's be realistic! There is no guarantee that the examiner will not repeat a topic. All I am saying is that the subject of status enquiries should be low on your list of priorities.

Your first job should be to draw up a complete list of past questions. Better still, you might like to make a list of topics from the syllabus and tick when that topic was last examined (exclude land, companies and cheques for the time being). Your list will look like this:

	5/92	10/91	5/91	10/90	5/90	10/89	5/89
Secrecy			√			√	√
Status enquiries		√					
Set-off							
Bankruptcy	√		√				√

Of the four topics shown, set-off would require special attention as a question had not been set for some time.

You can go back as far as you like. I suggest you go right back to April 1980.

You can now do a similar exercise in respect of land, companies and cheques, by breaking down those topics into as much detail as you want. Here's an example:

LAND

Basic (i.e., questions involving basic knowledge, e.g., October 1991 Q6).

Solicitors' undertakings (i.e., questions requiring a knowledge of how solicitors' undertakings are used, e.g., May 1990 Q6).

Others (i.e., any questions not falling into one of the above; the number will depend upon how much you have broken down the subject-matter).

COMPANIES

Account-opening procedure (e.g., September 1986 Q4(a)).

Companies House registrations (e.g., October 1988 Q7).

Wages and salaries (e.g., October 1991 Q4).

Floating charges (e.g., May 1991 Q7(b)).

CHEQUES

Negotiability (e.g., September 1985 Q4).

Paying banker (e.g., May 1992 Q3).

Collecting banker (e.g., October 1988 Q1(b)).

Holder for value (e.g., May 1991 Q4(a)).

Clearing system (e.g., October 1991 Q3(a)).

Let me repeat: there is no guarantee of the same topic not being examined at successive sittings. Indeed, if I were chief examiner I would do that occasionally to catch you out.

As a teacher, I tell my students that ideally the whole of the syllabus should be studied in detail. But we are not in an ideal situation. Your time is limited and precious. I'm trying to help you to use that time effectively in respect of a huge syllabus.

Information Sources

You can choose to study by attendance at college classes, by correspondence course or by studying privately. Whichever method you decide upon, it is vital that the information you receive is up to date. Things change so quickly that any written material is unlikely to be completely up to date from the first moment it is published. For example, there will be a new case to add a different slant to what has been learned.

Marks will be awarded in the exam if you can show that you are up to date. But how can you ensure that you keep abreast of developments? Here are a few suggestions:

(a) Bank circulars — obviously applies only to practising bankers. Changes in practice or procedure will be circularised throughout your bank.

(b) Newspapers — read the law reports in *The Times*.

(c) *Banking World* — the 'Courts' page and relevant 'Signpost' articles.

(d) *Updating Notes* — Don't forget to read the Law Relating to Banking notes also.

Examiners' reports are a vital source of information (but not for keeping up to date). As a teacher who relies heavily for his living on students wanting face-to-face tuition, I hate to admit that if students had a working knowledge of every question and answer set since April 1980, they would stand an excellent chance of passing. Some of the answers however would have to be amended to cater for legislation such as the Companies Act 1985 and the Insolvency Act 1986.

Finally, again for practising bankers, there is so much useful information within bank branches. If you can see the various security forms, Land Registry forms etc., it makes the world of difference to your understanding of how they are used. So, make a nuisance of yourself if necessary to see these things at first hand.

Examination Technique

Whereas familiarity with a mnemonic for the principles of lending will help students of the Lending paper to make relevant comments in lending questions, there is no easy formula for Branch Banking — Law and Practice. The nature and requirements of the questions vary so much that it is impossible to group them together under one convenient banner. Obviously there are useful formats that can form the basis of an answer but none can be applied across every type of question.

Two will be considered here: PERCY (or PERKS) and TIPS.

PERCY or PERKS

> P   PRINCIPLES
> E   EXCEPTIONS
> R   RELATE TO QUESTION
> C   CONCLUSION

The previous chief examiner, John Kelly, covered this format in his article in *Banking World*, April 1989. He has long advocated this system, and it works perfectly for some topics, such as secrecy. Usually, he gives the following example to illustrate the format:

A policeman walks into your branch and informs you of a major robbery in town. He asks for the addresses of any of your customers who have recently paid in an unusually large amount of new £10 notes. You recall such a customer. What should you do?

Principles

Bank's duty of secrecy — established in *Joachimson* case.

Exceptions

Four exceptions established in *Tournier* case:

  (a) Compulsion of law.
  (b) Interests of public.
  (c) Interests of bank.
  (d) Customer's express or implied consent.

Relate

Do any of these exceptions apply in this situation?

If yes, information can be given.

If no, bank must refuse request.

Compulsion of law? request from a policeman is not compulsion of law. A court order represents compulsion of law.

Interests of public? Possibly — dangerous however, if customer is innocent — bank unlikely to be sued, however, just for giving address in the circumstances.

Interests of Bank? In no way.

Customer's Express or Implied Consent? Certainly not!

Conclusion

Bank would claim public interest as justification for giving the address. Safer, however, to refuse altogether unless served with court order.

Exam questions

Let us now have a look at PERCY in action in actual examination questions:

Question 1

Nice Things Ltd is a fancy goods manufacturer borrowing £200,000 on current account, secured by a guarantee for £50,000 given by the main director and shareholder, Peter Jensen. This guarantee is supported by a legal charge over a Living Assurance Life Policy for £30,000, with a surrender value of £13,219, and a portfolio of stocks and shares with a market value of £18,278, lodged with a memorandum of deposit.

Mr Jensen calls to see you and confirms your fears that trade is bad. He tell you that, on his accountant's advice, he will be calling a meeting of creditors with a view to liquidation. He expects that assets will realise £300,000, although total liabilities are £900,000.

Mr Jensen says he would like to honour his guarantee liability straightaway, and he draws a cheque on his joint account at your branch, which has a credit balance of £56,218. He hands this cheque to you to pay into the company's account. He then asks you to place his life policy and share certificates in safe custody since you will no longer require them as security, and asks for the cancelled guarantee to be sent to his accountants, so that he can claim tax relief on the payment made.

Required:

State how you would handle this situation and the considerations you would have in mind. Give reasons for your answer.

(September 1984 Q7)

Principles

Guarantee is collateral security.

Proceeds should be placed to a securities realisation account so as to preserve the bank's claim against the company for the full debt (*Re Sass*).

Security taken in support of a guarantee can be used only to satisfy the guarantor's liability — it cannot be used to reduce the company debt.

Guarantee form is the bank's property and is never given up.

Exceptions

Proceeds of collateral security can be placed direct to the principal debtor's account when they are fully repaying the principal debt because the bank then has no reason to preserve the principal debtor's liability.

Relate

Guarantor's money does not fully repay company debt.

Therefore place £50,000 to securities realisation account.

Check joint account mandate to ensure 'Either to sign'.

Bank claims £200,000 in company liquidation.

Bank receives £66,667 (33p in £).

Plus guarantor's £50,000.

Bank loses £83,334.

Supporting security no longer relied upon.

Re-assign life policy (security document to remain with policy) — place in safe custody.

Memorandum of deposit over shares placed on cancelled documents file.

If equitable charge held over shares, certificate still in guarantor's name and can be placed in safe custody.

If legal charge held over shares, bank will be holding certificate in name of bank's nominees — need to be transferred back into guarantor's name before placing in safe custody.

Bank will retain guarantee form but a copy can be provided.

Conclusion

There is no conclusion to draw in this answer. Don't try to contrive one where it is not relevant.

Note

The question said the shares were lodged with a memorandum of deposit. Many people (justifiably in my opinion) would assume the bank had an equitable charge only. In a different question where shares were held under a memorandum of deposit, Mr Kelly, in his report, said that students should not make that assumption, because with a legal charge also, a memorandum of deposit would normally be held.

Question 2

Your customers, Short Time Ltd, have had an account with your bank for 12 years. You hold a mandate authorising withdrawals, provided cheques are signed by one director and the company secretary. Since the account was opened, Tom Short and Alan Short have remained directors, but the office of secretary has changed on two occasions, being held from 1974 until 1979 by James Duncan, from 1979 to 1984 by John Watson, and since 1984 by Geoffrey Hill.

Towards the end of last year the company discovered that when John Watson was secretary he had engaged in certain fraudulent activities. Further researches have shown, so Tom and Alan Short claim, that in the year 1983 the bank paid cheques, totalling about £60,000, on one signature only, that of John Watson. They also say that in 1984 you paid 17 cheques, totalling £17,000, which were signed by John Watson but on which the signature of one or other of the directors was forged. As it has been your practice to return paid cheques to the company, you cannot verify these statements within the branch.

A letter from the company's solicitors received today seeks reimbursement of £77,000 plus interest if legal action is to be avoided.

Required:

Comment on the bank's position, referring to any relevant statute or case law. State what defences you might raise in the hope of limiting any loss, and what the likelihood of success would be. Would you be prepared to meet the claim in full at once? Give reasons for your answer.

(September 1986 Q1)

PRINCIPLES

(a) Bank has paid cheques on one signature only — not in accordance with mandate.

Banks can only debit an account with customer's written authority (*Joachimson* case) — bank has no such authority.

(b) Bank has paid against forged drawer's signature.

Bills of Exchange Act 1882, s.24 makes this inoperative.

Therefore, again, bank has no authority to debit account.

Exceptions

(a) Bank might have a defence if cheques paid on one signature were in respect of legitimate company debts (*Liggett (Liverpool) Ltd* v *Barclays Bank*).

(b) Estoppel in respect of forged cheques, i.e., customer precluded from denying genuineness of signature where they knew of forgeries and did nothing about it (*Greenwood* v *Martins Bank; Brown* v *Westminster Bank*).

Relate

Bank will not meet claim without investigation.

Has company kept paid cheques? If so, inspect them to see that what they claim is correct.

On the assumption that claims are correct, then in respect of cheques with one signature, who are the payees?

If legitimate company debts, bank can resist claim for a refund, but apologise for paying on only one signature.

In respect of forged cheques, this is obvious fraud and therefore unlikely to refer to legitimate debts.

Bank's defence of estoppel is likely to fail also, as there is no indication that directors were aware of situation.

However, company has had statements. Any defence there? Should they have been aware?

Directors would be expected to be more aware than (say) an individual in respect of a personal account.

But customers not obliged to check statements (*Tai Hing Cotton Mill Ltd* v *Liu Chong Hing Bank Ltd*) — therefore bank has no defence re statements.

Conclusion

Assuming claim is correct, bank's only hope appears to be that some of cheques paid on one signature were in payment of legitimate debts.

No other defences.

TIPS

An alternative to PERCY is a mnemonic which was devised for the Institute's Branch Banking — Law and Practice video on exam technique:

    T   THINK
    I   ISSUES
    P   PROBLEMS
    S   SOLUTIONS

Think

It is vital that you think for at least five minutes before starting your answer. During this time you can start to map out your answer. Jot down the key points highlighted in the question. What are the issues, what problems are raised, how can they be solved? You can then write your answer under those headings, if you wish.

Issues

What issues are raised in the question? What is the question all about? What is the examiner getting at? What area of the syllabus are we in — secrecy, negotiability, bankruptcy etc? ('Issues' correspond closely with John Kelly's 'Principles and Exceptions'.)

Problems and Solutions

This is where I think TIPS has a slight advantage over PERCY for 'problem-type' questions. The mnemonic emphasises the problems — there might be more than one. For each problem there might be more than one possible solution.

Don't think that there is always a right and wrong answer in problem questions. The bank might be on a hiding to nothing in that whichever solution the bank selects could have potential dangers, and the bank simply chooses the lesser of two evils.

Exam questions

Let us now look at two exam questions, one from each section, and apply TIPS to them.

Question 1

You have agreed to lend to your customer, Mr Kirby, £12,000 on a fluctuating current account, to help with working capital for his tailoring business. As security you have asked Mr Kirby for a legal mortgage over his domestic property, which Mr Kirby now values at £30,000. However, when the property was acquired by Mr Kirby, he was assisted to the extent of £10,000 by a friend, with whom he lodged the land certificate as security. The friend, Mr A. Smith, acting on his solicitor's advice, lodged a notice of deposit at the Land Registry, to protect his position.

Are there likely to be any special problems with the security offered, and, if so, what can be done to overcome them? Give reasons for your answer.

(September 1981 Q7(a))

Think

Take five minutes to jot down the issues, problems and possible solutions to those problems. Cross out your notes as you cover them in your answer.

Issues

The first mortgage is equitable — land certificate and notice of deposit.

Land certificate has to be produced to District Land Registry every time there is a disposition of the land (Land Registration Act 1925, s.64).

Creation of legal mortgage is regarded as a disposition.

Secondly, the property might be matrimonial property — if there is a Mrs Kirby she might be able to exercise occupational rights (*Williams & Glyn's Bank Ltd* v *Boland*).

Problems and Solutions

Bank will not be able to register a legal mortgage because Land Registry will not issue a charge certificate whilst the equitable mortgagee has possession of the land certificate.

Bank needs to ask Smith to register his charge by exchanging land certificate for a charge certificate.

Bank can then register its charge.

Smith might refuse because of registration fees.

Bank can offer to pay these, debiting customer.

If Smith is still unhelpful, bank could register a caution but this only means that the bank would be informed of any intended dealings.

As a last resort, bank could offer to pay off equitable mortgage in order to gain possession of land certificate.

The problem of a Mrs Kirby with occupational rights is that she might prevent the bank from exercising its power of sale.

Bank would need to get her to postpone her rights by signing a suitable clause on the charge form.

Question 2

One of your customers, Alan Heath, calls in a perplexed state to seek your advice. He says that he has just received a letter from a firm of solicitors, Sew & Co., which states that they act for a Mr Malcolm Dobson and that on behalf of their client, they claim £800 from Mr Heath, being the sum due by him on a cheque which he issued, numbered 127892 and dated 17 July 1985. Mr Heath says he has never heard of Malcolm Dobson, but he recalls issuing and then stopping a cheque for £800 last July, but that this was payable to Robert Tait and was the payment for a hi-fi unit which he had bought but which proved to be defective.

On examining your returned cheque register you are able to confirm that on 21 July 1985 cheque number 127892 was returned to the presenting bank with the answer 'payment stopped by order of drawer'.

Required:

State how you would explain the reasons for the solicitor's letter. Say if you can advise Mr Heath, and if so, how. Is there any other advice you could give him?

(September 1985 Q4)

Think

Again, think for five minutes, jotting down issues, problems and solutions before starting your answer.

Issues

Major issue is negotiability.

Cheque negotiated by Tait to Dobson.

The essence of negotiability is that a transferee can obtain better rights to a cheque than the transferor had.

Dobson might be a holder in due course (Bills of Exchange Act 1882, s.29).

Two things destroy negotiability — a 'not negotiable' crossing or a forged endorsement.

Problems and Solutions

Dobson might be able to enforce payment against the drawer (Heath) as a holder in due course.

Heath needs to see the cheque to see if it was crossed 'not negotiable' — if it was, claim can be defeated.

Is Tait's endorsement genuine? It probably is.

It would be wise for Heath to seek legal advice.

A solicitor could advise Heath of his rights and any counter claims.

Situation could not have arisen if cheque had been crossed 'not negotiable'.

Advise Heath to do this in future.

Comparison of PERCY and TIPS

It could be argued that if you wanted to apply PERCY rigidly, the answer to the Kirby-question would have been:

Principles: Land Registry will not issue a Charge Certificate until they have the Land Certificate.
Exceptions: None.
Relate: Bank cannot get legal charge.
Conclusion: Bank cannot lend.

This approach would be extreme and nobody would dream of applying any formula as rigidly as that — would they? Hopefully, under the heading of 'Relate', the problems and possible solutions would have been discussed. Indeed, if either of the formulae is used flexibly, it can be applied to any question.

So, where does this leave you? Can you handle two separate formulae depending on the type of question? Can you use just one of them, and remember to use it flexibly? To confuse matters even further, don't forget that some questions require no exam technique at all. They are just a test of technical knowledge. Here is an example:

Question 3

David and Thelma Evans bank at your branch. You hold a joint account mandate in their names, dated 3 March 1982, allowing either to sign and incorporating joint and several liability. As security for an overdraft of £19,000, your customers agreed to lodge the deeds relating to their matrimonial home valued at £65,000. When they call with the deeds, you examine them and give David and Thelma a receipt on a schedule for all the documents, which include an abstract of title, a conveyance and local searches. The conveyance, dated 17 June 1985, transfers the title to David Evans and Thelma Evans from the previous owner Tony Williams. As the lending is to be short term, you have agreed to rely on the informal deposit of the deeds and no mortgage papers will be signed.

Required:

Answer the following questions in respect of your securities formalities. In all cases, give reasons for your answer:

(a) Should you register your security as a C(i) entry at the Land Charges Register?

(b) Should you register your security as a C(iii) entry at the Land Charges Register?

(c) Should you register your security as a caution at the Land Registry?

(d) Should you search the Land Charges Register at the Land Charges Department at any time? If so, against which names should you search and why?

(e) Should you search the Land Registry at any time? If you did, what would you require from your customer to facilitate this search?

(f) What should you bear in mind about the fire insurance covering the property? What should you do, if anything, in relation to this aspect of the transaction?

(September 1986 Q6)

With these questions, you just get on with it!

The trouble with any formula is that, unless you are careful, you get too obsessed with *how* you are saying something as opposed to *what* you are saying. You can spend five minutes worrying over whether a certain point is a principle or an exception, or an issue or a problem.

With that in mind, I suggest a third alternative which can be used for any question.

(a) THINK — you certainly need to spend at least five minutes thinking, and planning your answer.

(b) PLAN — during the five minutes thinking time, jot down what the question is about, what issues are raised, what cases are relevant, what statute(s) need to be mentioned. Is there a principle to be applied or does the question raise problems which need to be solved? When you have done that, then you start the answer.

(c) ANSWER — in tabulated form. Cross off the points in your plan as you cover them in your answer. Ensure that you cover all the points, and then cross out the whole of the plan.

(d) REVIEW — try to leave a minute or two to review the answer, either immediately, or to accumulate for a review of all the answers at the end.

I know what you're thinking. Why didn't I say that at the beginning? Simply because I knew that the two previous formulae were well documented — indeed I was instrumental in the birth of TIPS. I'm also aware, from my teaching experience, that unless a student is capable of using either formula flexibly, then both become more of a hindrance than a help.

So, I felt obliged to go through both formats, give you my own thoughts and leave the final decision to you.

Revision

Just as your study of the subject matter needs to be prioritised, then so does your revision. The worst type of revision is to sit down with a textbook or your notes, and just read. You'll be lucky if you are still awake 10 minutes later. Even if you manage an hour, the *effective* time will be much less. Are you seriously trying to tell me that your mind will not have wandered to more pleasant thoughts?

Remember — your time is short and precious — so don't waste it.

Here are a few hints to liven up your revision.

Brainstorming

Select a subject and write down, as briefly as possible, all you can remember about that subject — facts, cases, statutes etc. It is vital that you actually write it down!

Spend no more than two minutes doing this — then check against your textbook or notes to see what you forgot. You will then be reading with a purpose which is much more interesting than the aimless exercise it otherwise would have been.

This exercise is even more beneficial if it can be done in pairs or groups.

Quizzes

There are many variations on this theme. As part of a group, you can make up questions for each other. The setting of questions is a most effective way of revising.

Apart from traditional quiz questions, you could have some really tough ones, e.g., a cases quiz. Draw up a list of cases from a textbook index, for example, and see if you can state their significance, for example:

Q. What principle was established in *Re Mechanisations (Eaglescliffe) Ltd* (1964)?

A. That registration of a debenture at Companies House was effective notice of all the clauses contained in the debenture.

Remember that quoting relevant cases earns marks, and therefore this could be a very worthwhile exercise.

Past questions

Hopefully you will have done written answers to past questions as part of your study of the subject. Do as many as you can at the revision stage also. The more written practice you get, the better! You can check out your answer against the relevant examiner's report, most of which give a detailed breakdown of what was required.

Do the answers under strict exam conditions! You're fooling only yourself if you don't.

Revision courses

If there is a convenient revision course, you will find attendance extremely beneficial — especially at one run by the Institute.

For those studying privately or by correspondence, it will be an ideal opportunity to bounce around ideas and to clear up points of detail. It will probably be your only opportunity for face-to-face discussion with an experienced tutor, and with other students. Those attending college classes will benefit from hearing it from someone different. A slightly different emphasis can help in the understanding of many points.

Conclusion

You should never sit down with a book with the intention of just reading (say) 10 pages or for (say) half an hour. You will achieve nothing. Read in order to check out specific points.

Final Words

I've left until last, one or two general comments which apply to all examinations, not just Branch Banking — Law and Practice. Nevertheless, they need to be said.

Last minute cramming

Personally, I don't believe in it! I never used to open a book on the day of the exam. I took the view that if I didn't know it now,

I never would. I used to try to relax and think of anything but the exam.

Try to think of the worst possible tragedy which could happen to you tomorrow. Suddenly the taking of a silly exam falls into perspective.

I know that it's all down to an individual's personal preferences. Many people can tell stories of revising a certain topic on the way to the exam, and sure enough, there it was on the question paper. But the chances are that that individual could have answered the question anyway. And for every such case, there are 99 who revise just before the exam, and the question does *not* come up.

So, my advice is — don't do it! It causes only confusion. In most cases, it does more harm than good.

Discipline your time

I know you're tired of hearing it, but: make sure you answer FIVE questions fully! Don't go overboard on your strong topics at the expense of doing only four.

It's difficult enough to get 51 marks out of 100, never mind 51 out of 80. If you did only one question in either Section B or C, then, with the section pass requirement, you would need to score 16 out of 20 for that question.

Which order?

Ideally you should do the compulsory question first. After that, it doesn't really matter what order you choose because you must do four *full* answers from Sections B and C to stand a realistic chance of passing.

Should you do your strongest question first? Most people recommend it in order to build up confidence. The potential problem is that you go overboard and take up too much time, thus causing pressure later on. Personally, I used to leave my strongest question until later — but you must make up your own mind.

Legibility

Try to be as neat as the situation allows you to be! I know there's a lot of nervous tension, but if the examiner cannot read what you've written, he can't give you the marks.

Planning your answer should help when it comes to writing it out, as you will not be thinking as you are writing. Remember also your tabulation! Long answers are not required, so you can afford to take a little more care in your presentation.

PART 3

Suggested Answers to Examination Questions

Before reading on, you might find it beneficial to re-read part 2 on examination technique. You will recall that two formulae were examined, and that I suggested that the best elements of both could be incorporated by simply planning your answer for five minutes, during which time you would note the main points to be brought out when you wrote out the answer.

I will now go through both the October 1991 and the May 1992 papers and you will see how questions often involve a principle or principles which, if not followed, lead to problems for the bank to which solutions must be found.

October 1991 Q1

(a) As the new Manager of Green Bank, you have today received a letter from Messrs Brooke, Owen and Co, solicitors, concerning your customer, Christopher Dowson. It appears that in July 1991 your predecessor gave a favourable reply to a status enquiry and that, on the strength of this reply, the solicitors obtained a garnishee summons naming Christopher Dowson as defendant. The summons proved unsuccessful since, on the date it was served on your branch, Mr Dowson's account was overdrawn.

The solicitors have now established that Mr Dowson's account was also overdrawn at the time of making their original enquiry. They are also aware that you recently made formal demand on Mr Dowson for repayment of his overdraft in the sum of £685. Accordingly, they are accusing the bank of both negligence and fraudulent misrepresentation in the framing of its reply, and claim repayment of their costs.

Required:

Comment, with reasons, on the bank's position. Discuss what defences, if any, the bank might put forward in response to the accusations made by the solicitors. (10)

(b) You have agreed to provide your customer, Edmund Blunden, with a loan of £10,000 to enable him to purchase some antique furniture. Your security will be an unlimited guarantee from his uncle, Edward Thomas.

The guarantee is to be supported and you are offered legal charges over the following investment holdings owned by Mr. Thomas:
- 10,000 Save and Prosper UK Equity Units;
- a promissory note for £5,000 signed by a wealthy local businessman and due for payment on 31 December 1992;
- 135 General Motors shares of common stock (US$) held in a good marking name.

Required:

Set out, in note form, the formalities necessary for taking each item of security. (10)

Suggested answer

Part (a)

The fact that the account was overdrawn when the reply was given does not mean that a good report cannot be given – that would imply that all borrowers were bad.

The fact that demand for repayment has been made does, however, suggest that the reply was too generous unless the position has deteriorated suddenly and unexpectedly since July.

Bank will have to look closely at position in July to determine whether reply was accurate.

If accurate, then no liability for bank.

If not accurate, bank has been careless/negligent/fraudulent and the claim should be met.

Possible defences for bank:

(a) Disclaimer clause – protected against negligence in *Hedley Byrne & Co. Ltd* v *Heller & Partners Ltd* (1963), but probably no longer effective as a result of the Unfair Contract Terms Act (1977) – did not protect against fraudulent misrepresentation in *Commercial Banking Co. of Sydney Ltd* v *R H Brown & Co.* (1972).

(b) Reply not signed – s.6 Statute of Frauds Amendment Act 1828 requires fraudulently misrepresented statements to be signed although this defence was not allowed in the *Commercial Banking Co. of Sydney* case.

Part (b)

This lending would be regulated by the Consumer Credit Act 1974.

Therefore, the guarantee would cover this advance only. Status enquiry on guarantor needed – updated regularly. Bank's guarantee form to be completed.

Is independent legal advice necessary for guarantor? Guarantor signs and receives copy of form.

(i) *Unit Trusts*

Mr Thomas must sign form of renunciation on reverse of certificate.

Security then transferred into name of bank's nominee company to complete legal charge.

(ii) *Promissory Note*

This is a negotiable instrument. Cannot be used as security – s.123 Consumer Credit Act.

(iii) *Shares*

Marking name will need to have endorsed certificate. Nothing else to do.

(iv) *General*

Bank will take memorandum of deposit. Securities will be valued and value updated at intervals.

Comment

Part (a) required a balanced discussion of the problems which can arise with replies to status enquiries and the possible solutions available to the bank.

Part (b) was procedural.

October 1991 Q2

(a) Recently your customer, Harold Monro, returned some unused American dollar travellers' cheques which he had previously purchased through your branch in advance of a trip to New York. After conversion, the sterling equivalent of £585 was credited to his account.

It subsequently transpired that the wrong exchange rate had been used and that Mr Monro's account had been overcredited with the sum of £165. His account was, therefore, debited with this amount and Mr Monro was sent a letter of apology with an advice of the adjustment that had been made.

Today, Mr Munro calls to see you. He complains that the bank should not have made such a mistake and, since he has spent the money, was not entitled to debit his account in the way it had done. He goes on to say that, unless the bank recredits his account with £165, he will complain to the Banking Ombudsman.

Required:

State how you would deal with this situation and the considerations you would have in mind. Give reasons for your answer.

(10)

(b) You have at your branch the account of William Cowper. Today, with credit balances of £196 on his current account and £4,250 on his high interest cheque account, you receive a visit from his daughter, Mrs Browning. She tells you that her father died last week in hospital.

Mrs Browning informs you that there is no will and that she is the sole surviving relative, her mother having died several years earlier. Also. since her father's only assets are the deposits at your branch, she has been advised by a solicitor that she need not take out letters of administration. She therefore asks you to transfer the balances of her late father's account to her own account, which you establish is maintained at a local branch of your bank.

Required:

State, with reasons. how you would react to this approach and, if you are prepared to release the funds, the steps you would take to ensure the bank is fully protected.

(10)

Suggested answer

Part (a)

There is much case law on this topic, e.g., *Lloyds Bank* v *Brooks* (1950).

Much of the confusion was cleared up by the case *United Overseas Bank* v *Jiwani* (1976), when it was established that in order for a customer to retain money wrongly credited, the following conditions had to apply:

(i) Bank has misrepresented state of account (this is undoubtedly so in this instance).

(ii) Customer was misled by the misrepresentation, i.e. did he know he had been over-credited? In the question much would depend on how familiar customer was with the correct exchange rate.

(iii) As a result of the misrepresentation, the customer has changed his position to such an extent that it would now be inequitable to have to repay (this would be difficult for customer to convince the Ombudsman about and, in any case, the bank is likely to be co-operative by offering an interest-free loan, if necessary, since it is the bank's error).

In the circumstances, it is unlikely that the Ombudsman would uphold the customer's claim.

Part (b)

If the value of a deceased's estate is less than £5,000, banks will release balances to the next of kin without probate or letters of administration (Administration of Estates (Small Payments) Act 1976).

Bank would need to see copy of death certificate. Safe custody records would be checked to ensure no will is held.

Deceased's account will be stopped.

Cheques will be returned 'drawer deceased'.

Bank needs proof of Mrs Browning's identity – check with solicitor which she mentioned, or with branch where her account is held.

Solicitor could also confirm her right to the money.

If satisfied, bank will release balances against her indemnity – money could be released via solicitor.

Comment

Legal knowledge and practical application were present in equal measure.

October 1991 Q3

(a) You are Manager of a branch of Gamma Bank, a settlement member of the Cheque and Credit Clearing Co. Ltd. James Stephens maintains an unsatisfactory account at your branch and you only allow him to draw against balances on his account if they represent cleared funds.

On Monday 14 October, when the cleared balance on his account was £16, James paid into his account a cheque for £175. The cheque was sent for clearance in the normal way.

On Friday 18 October, James called to withdraw the sum of £180. The cashier paid him this amount after having first established within the branch that the cheque for £175 had not been returned unpaid.

Today, Monday 21 October, the cheque for £175 was returned in the post with the answer 'refer to drawer'. The accompanying advice was dated 17 October.

Your cashier wants you to refuse the return of the cheque on the basis that the paying bank has failed to adhere to the Clearing House Rules for late returns.

Required:

(i) Discuss Gamma Bank's position and state whether you agree with your cashier's views. (10)

(ii) State how the situation would have differed, if at all, if the cheque had been returned with the answer 'post dated'. (2)

Give reasons for your answers.

(b) Today, you receive a visit from Ralph Hodgson. He tells you that he is a student, aged 17, and the son of Henry Hodgson, a construction engineer. Henry Hodgson has both current and savings accounts at your branch; in addition, you are holding a number of share certificates and sealed envelopes on Henry's behalf in safe custody.

Ralph informs you that his father has had to go to the Far East on urgent business and will be away for at least six months. In his absence, he has appointed Ralph as his attorney.

Ralph produces a copy of the power of attorney and you notice that this has been drawn up in accordance with Section 10 of the Powers of Attorney Act, 1971. He requests a cheque book for his father's current account together with a list of the items held in safe custody. He also asks if he can arrange for his mother to sign on the account since he is shortly going to university and there will be regular household bills needing to be paid.

Required:

State how you would deal with this situation and the considerations you would have in mind. Give reasons for your answer.

(8)

Suggested answer

Part (a)(i)

Banks are expected to either pay or return cheques on the day of presentation.

Under the inadvertence rule, banks are allowed to return cheques on the day after presentation so long as the reason for return is not a technical irregularity.

If the cheque is for over £500, the bank must telephone its intentions to the collecting bank before 12 noon.

Since the amount was less than £500, there was no need to telephone and, therefore, the collecting bank must accept the late return.

There has been a delay in the post but that is of no help to the collecting bank.

Collecting bank must try to recover funds from customer or attempt to enforce payment against drawer as a holder in due course but, since cheque has been returned for lack of funds, this is not likely to be successful.

Part (a)(ii)

'Post dated' is a technical irregularity and, therefore, the collecting bank does not have to accept the late return.

Collecting bank will debit drawer bank unless drawer bank can show that cheque was not presented until 17 October (unlikely).

Part (b)

A minor can act as an attorney.

Bank will prefer to see the original of the power of attorney.

Proof of Ralph's identity will be needed, plus specimen signature.

Powers drawn under s.10 permit an attorney to do anything which the donor could lawfully do.

Cheque book and a list of safe custody items can be given to Ralph.

An attorney is not allowed to delegate power to someone else (unless the original document permits it) and, therefore, Ralph's mother cannot sign on the account.

Ralph could sign standing orders for the bills.

Comment

Part (a) required careful application of the inadvertence rule, paying particular attention to the dates. Branch bankers should not have had any problems with this as it is seen so often in practice. Part (b) involved something which is not seen so often and knowledge of s.10 was essential to get good marks.

October 1991 Q4

At your branch you have the account of E Pound Ltd, building contractors. The company has two directors and 15 full-time employees. In addition, it is currently employing six workers as sub-contractors on a labour-only basis.

Recently the company has been experiencing trading difficulties and, with effect from the week beginning Monday 24 June 1991, you have been operating a separate wages and salaries account. The first week's wages totalling £2,500 were debited to the account on Thursday 27 June 1991.

Today, 21 October, you notice from the morning print-out that the borrowing on the wages and salaries account has reduced by £2,500 to £40,000. Also, in the morning post is a letter from the company secretary stating that the balance of £40,000 is currently made up as follows:

Directors' remuneration	£1,600
Employees' wages	£24,000
Advances to sub-contracted workers	£14,400

Required:

(a) Explain the advantages to a bank of opening a separate wages and salaries account for a limited company, and state briefly whether these advantages would apply if you were dealing with the account of either a sole trader or a partnership.   (10)

(b) Discuss the operation to date of the wages and salaries account of E Pound Ltd, and state what steps, if any, you would take to remedy any shortcomings that might exist.   (10)

Give reasons for your answers.

Suggested answer

Part (a)

Under Schedule 6 of the Insolvency Act 1986, unpaid wages and salaries of employees rank as a preferential debt.

The maximum period is four months and the maximum amount is currently £800 per employee.

If a bank lends to pay wages and salaries, then the bank is a preferential creditor.

Lending can be done on current account but *Clayton's* case will reduce the preferential debt.

It is better to operate a separate account to avoid *Clayton's* case and also to monitor the position more easily.

Also, if the bank is secured, the process of security might be used to repay non-preferential debt as in *Re William Hall (Contractors) Ltd* (1967).

Since the Insolvency Act, wages and salaries of employees in sole traders and partnerships are treated as preferential debts.

Part (b)

The balance of wages and salaries account should always reflect the last 16 weeks' wages (four-month period) – hence the transfer from the current account repaying the first week's wages.

In this instance, other items have been debited to the wages account also – the company should immediately make a transfer from the current account to eliminate directors' remuneration and advances to sub-contracted workers which are not preferential debts.

Also, the company has only 15 employees – the maximum amount per employee allowed as preferential debt is £800.

Therefore, the bank needs to ensure that, in future, the balance of the wages account should not exceed £12,000 (15 x £800) and should not contain non-preferential items.

At the moment wages amount to £24,000. The company should make a transfer of £12,000 from the current account to reduce the wages account to £12,000. Therefore, the total transfer required from the current account is £28,000.

Comment

This question contained a combination of detached legal requirements and the application of those requirements to ensure that the bank is always in the most advantageous position. As stated earlier, the subject is a 'knowledge' subject and without it candidates have no chance of passing.

October 1991 Q5

Your customer, Lionel Johnson, is overdrawn £16,000 and you have asked him to provide security. He called to see you last week and you have agreed to take the following:

(a) a second mortgage over his house. Mr Johnson has advised you that the house is currently worth £75,000 and that his employer, from whom he has a loan of £40,000 on preferential terms, is the first mortgagee;

(b) a legal assignment over a life policy, nominal value £10,000, which according to Mr Johnson has a surrender value of £2,000.

Today you are approached by your security clerk. He tells you that, having made the usual enquiries of Mr Johnson's employers, he has established that Mr Johnson's house is on registered land and that the employer holds the land certificate protected by a notice of deposit. Also, Mr Johnson has recently telephoned to say that he will be unable to produce the life policy document since this went missing some time ago, a fact which had slipped his memory when he spoke to you last week.

Required:

State the effect of these developments on the security arrangements as proposed and, in regard to the securities, discuss the possible options now available to the bank. Give reasons for your answers. (20)

Suggested answer

Part (a)

The first mortgage is equitable – the employer is holding land certificate supported by notice of deposit. This creates a problem for the bank.

The bank will not be able to register a charge unless the first mortgagee registers his charge – under s.64 Land Registration Act 1925, the land certificate is required by the Land Registry before it will register a charge – the land certificate is in the hands of the first mortgagee.

The bank has a number of alternative solutions.

Ask first mortgagee to register charge – the bank will offer to pay registration fees – then the bank can also register.

If the first mortgagee is unwilling to register, the bank can place a caution on the register. This is not a charge but at least the bank will be advised of any intended dealings involving the property.

The bank could pay off the first mortgage but this is at a preferential rate and the bank is unlikely to want to do this.

Part (b)

The bank is still able to take an assignment without the policy but failure to produce it amounts to constructive notice of a previous assignment (*Spencer* v *Clarke* (1878)).

The policies of the Assurance Act (1867) states that priority between assignees is determined by the date notice of assignment is given to the insurance company.

This implies that if the bank gave notice and no previous notice had been received by the insurance company, then the bank's priority would be safe. Unfortunately, the decision in *Newman* v *Newman* (1885) overruled the Act. Therefore, the bank cannot get priority by giving notice over a previous assignee who has not given notice.

It will, however, get priority over subsequent assignees and be advised of any intended surrender of the policy.

If there is a previous assignee, who has not given notice, the bank will not be able to advise him of the bank's assignment, and the first assignee could make further advances reducing the value of the bank's security.

Duplicate policies can be issued by insurance companies but usually only against a banker's indemnity; the bank runs the risk of having to pay out against the indemnity in the future when it may no longer be in touch with the customer.

The bank has to be completely satisfied with the customer's integrity before going ahead on this basis.

Comment

This is the perfect example of the 'problem-type' question. There is no convenient procedural list. Candidates have to think through the problems and come up with workable solutions. If part (a) sounds familiar, a similar question was asked in September 1981 and is used earlier in the book to illustrate examination techniques.

October 1991 Q6

Prufrock Ltd, a textile company, has maintained a satisfactory credit account at your branch for several years. Expanding business has, however, made it essential for the company to install additional plant at a total cost of £75,000. Part of the cost can be met from cash resources but there will be a cash shortfall of £20,000.

Recently Mr Eliot, the Finance Director, called to see you to discuss ways in which this cash shortfall might be financed. He explained that the company was not prepared to charge trading assets, nor were the directors attracted to the idea of leasing or hire purchase. However, you learn that 18 months ago the company sold a piece of freehold unregistered land to an associated company, Burbank Ltd, for £40,000. This sum is being repaid over eight years at an annual rate of £5,000 and Prufrock Ltd has a legal mortgage over the land in question. The first repayment was made on 1 April 1991.

You therefore suggest to Mr Eliot that, if Prufrock Ltd will charge its legal mortgage to the bank, you will make available to the company a loan of £20,000 repayable over four years.

After referring back to his fellow directors, Mr Eliot today telephones and accepts your offer.

Required:

(a) Describe the type of security being offered and explain, with reasons, the steps and precautions necessary to take and perfect a valid charge.   (17)

(b) With this type of security, state what rights the bank might exercise if the loan is not repaid as arranged.   (3)

Suggested answer

Part (a)

The type of security is a sub-mortgage.

The security value of a sub-mortgage is not the market value of the property but the amount outstanding on the original mortgage.

When Burbank has repaid its loan to Prufrock, the title deeds have to be returned to Burbank. Therefore, bank lending to Prufrock has to be less than the amount of the original mortgage and for no longer than the period of the original mortgage.

The bank has to be sure that Prufrock's mortgage is legally correct. It has to:

– obtain deeds from Prufrock;

– ensure from Burbank's memorandum and articles that company and directors' powers were not exceeded (some banks no longer concern themselves with this aspect);

- ensure mortgage form was correctly executed and registered at Companies House within 21 days (s.395 Companies Act 1985);

- ensure searches done at Companies House at the Land Charges Registry (clear searches);

- ensure notice was given to fire insurance company and that cover is adequate;

- confirm amount of original mortgage and repayment details.

The bank can then go ahead with taking the sub-mortgage. It needs to:

- get professional valuation of property to ensure it is not less than amount of original mortgage;

- get report on title done;

- check Prufrock's memorandum and articles for company and directors' powers (not all banks);

- ensure Burbank are good for repayment of original mortgage as this will be the source of repayment of Prufrock's loan;

- execute sub-mortgage form;

- register at Companies House within 21 days;

- carry out searches (Companies House, LCR or local authority) to ensure there are no prior charges or interests – some could have been registered since the date of the original mortgage;

- give notice to fire insurance company;

- give notice to Burbank and ensure that all future mortgage repayments come direct to bank – confirm amount outstanding – obtain acknowledgement of notice;

- lend on separate account and reduce limit and value of security by each instalment received.

Part (b)

The bank's rights are determined by whether it is Prufrock or Burbank which defaults.

If it is Prufrock, the bank has no rights against Burbank or the property; the bank can sue Prufrock and sell sub-mortgage.

If Burbank defaults on original mortgage, the bank has all the rights against the property that Prufrock has.

Comment

A straight procedural question although the security value of sub-mortgages required special attention.

October 1991 Q7

Mr Robert Frost has a current account at your branch. There is also a current account in the name of his wife, Mary. Mary Frost, whom you have never met, owns shares in a number of different companies, and the certificates are held by you in safe custody.

Recently Mr Frost, who runs an antique stall in the local market, approached you for a loan of £30,000 to enable him to purchase some items at auction. You agreed to assist subject to a guarantee from Mrs Frost supported by a legal charge over her shares to a value of £40,000.

Mr Frost subsequently called at your branch with a lady whom he introduced as his wife. She signed the security and stock transfer forms, and a respected local solicitor, who had been called in by Mr Frost for the purpose, witnessed her signature. The solicitor also added to each charge form a certificate stating, 'I certify that I have explained the nature and purpose of the within document to Mary Frost and that she has signed under her own free will'.

In due course, the completed stock exchange transfer forms were submitted to the appropriate company registrars and the shares transferred into the name of the bank's nominee company.

Mr Frost then withdrew the amount of the loan and disappeared. It has subsequently transpired that the lady in question was not Mrs Frost and that the signature on the security and stock transfer forms bore no resemblance to that of the real Mrs Frost.

Required:

(a) Giving reasons for your answers, discuss the respective positions of:
(i)   Mrs Frost;
(ii) the local solicitor;
(iii) the company registrars;
(iv) the bank.

(15)

(b) Indicate what steps, if any, the bank should now take.

(5)

Suggested answer

Part (a)

(i)   *Mrs Frost*
She has been defrauded and is obviously not responsible. The forged transfer is invalid. She is entitled to full restoration of her previous position.

(ii)   *Solicitor*
A respected local solicitor is unlikely to be party to the deception. His role is merely to give independent legal advice to whom he believes to be Mrs Frost. He would not be expected to check her identity.

It would have been the bank which insisted on independent legal advice and, therefore, the solicitor is merely confirming there was no undue influence.

(iii)   *Company Registrars*
In two cases, the principle has been upheld that parties submitting transfer forms to company registrars impliedly represent that the transferor's signature is genuine:

> *Sheffield Corporation* v *Barclays* (1905)
> *Yeng and Another* v *Hongkong & Shanghai Banking Corporation* (1980)

The bank is impliedly indemnifying the company against loss.

(iv) *Bank*

The bank is liable and will have to stand the loss unless the culprits can be traced.

Part (b)

- Bank will have to transfer shares back into Mrs Frost's name; costs will be covered by bank.

- Guarantee will be cancelled.

- Apology given to Mrs Frost – tell her that her position has been restored.

- Advise police via fraud office.

- Write off loan of £30,000 unless culprits can be found.

Comment

Application of knowledge and common sense were called for in this question. It was originally asked during the 1970s, so it might profit candidates to look back a long way for potential questions.

May 1992 Q1

Robert Abel is a valued customer at your branch. Four years ago you lent him £20,000 on loan account to acquire a partnership in a local firm of accountants. Repayment was agreed at a rate of £4,000 per annum, and the loan was secured by a guarantee from his mother supported by an equitable charge over stock exchange securities, current value £28,000. The borrowing is being repaid as arranged and the latest accounts of the partnership, which also banks at your branch, show good profits being made.

Today, you receive a letter from Mr Abel enclosing a cheque for £10,642 issued by a firm of stockbrokers. He tells you that the money is from the sale of some recently inherited shares. Mr Abel asks you to credit the funds to his current account and, following clearance of the cheque, to repay the loan. Once this is done, he requests that you write to his mother confirming her immediate release from the guarantee liability, and returning her share certificates.

Your clerk is reluctant to agree to Mr Abel's request on the grounds that a preference may have taken place.

Required:

  (a) State what you understand by the term 'preference'.

                                                       (2)

  (b) Outline the criteria in respect of which any claim for preference against an individual is judged.   (6)

  (c) Having regard to your clerk's comments, discuss fully the considerations you would have in mind in dealing with Mr Abel's request and explain what action you would take. Give reasons for your answer.   (12)

Suggested answer

Part (a)

A preference occurs when a company or an individual does something which puts someone else, (for example a creditor or a guarantor) into an advantageous position in the event of the insolvency of the company or individual. There are time limits involved.

Part (b)

Where individuals are concerned, preferences are dealt with in ss.340 and 341 of the Insolvency Act 1986.

Section 340 states that an individual must be influenced by a desire to put the beneficiary of the action into a better position. If the beneficiary is an associate of the individual, this desire is presumed by the court, unless the contrary is shown.

Section 341 states that the preference has to occur in the six-month period prior to the presentation of the petition (or two years if an associate is involved).

Section 341 also states that the individual has to be insolvent at the time of the preference or become insolvent as a result of the preference.

The onus is on the trustee in bankruptcy to prove these facts.

Part (c)

In the situation in question, it could be argued that the bank is being preferred (non-associate) or the mother (associate).

A relative is defined as an associate in s.435 of the Insolvency Act.

If the bank suspected preference, it would be entitled to refuse to release the guarantor from liability and refuse to release the share certificates until the danger has passed.

But is there a risk of Robert Abel going bankrupt in the foreseeable future?

- The loan is being repaid as expected.
- The partnership is profitable.
- There seems to be no risk of imminent bankruptcy.

He is a valued customer and there is no reason to doubt that the source of the funds is not as he says.

If in doubt the bank could ask for confirmation of the inheritance but that could imply mistrust of the customer and not worth risking the goodwill.

The bank would do as Mr Abel asks, that is, write to the mother, and then put the guarantee form on the cancelled documents file and get a receipt for the share certificates.

If, surprisingly, bankruptcy did follow, and the bank had to refund the preference monies, the bank could apply to court, under s.342, to restore its position to what it was.

Comment

Parts (a) and (b) were factual. Part (c) presented the 'trap' of suspecting preference when the circumstances suggested there was little risk of bankruptcy following. Preferences are a danger only if the customer's financial position suggests the possibility of bankruptcy.

May 1992 Q2

Discuss the bank's position in regard to each of the following situations, and explain what action you would take. Give reasons for your answers.

(a) Thomas Hayward has an unsatisfactory account at your branch and his overdraft, which is unsecured, presently stands at £852.

For a number of weeks you have been trying, unsuccessfully, to obtain Mr Hayward's proposals for repayment of the borrowing, and you recently advised him that, unless the account was placed in credit by the end of May, you would call up the outstanding debt.

Today, you receive a letter from Mr Hayward enclosing a cheque for £900. He asks you to collect the cheque and, assuming it is paid, to use the funds to meet a cheque for £895 which he has drawn on his account in favour of Albert Ward. (6)

(b) One of your staff draws your attention to the account of the executors of W Rhodes deceased, which was opened in March 1991. The usual bank mandate was taken, and this provides for any one of the three executors to sign on the account.

It is suggested that you write to the executors pointing out that, since the account has been opened for longer than one year, a new mandate must be completed requiring all three to sign on the account in future. (7)

(c) Your valued customer, Tom Richardson & Co. Ltd, appears to be using a cheque book prepared by the bank and mistakenly styled Tom Richardson & Co. The company has an annual turnover of £850,000, and maintains substantial credit balances on current account.   (7)

Suggested answer

Part (a)

The principle involved is appropriation.

The rules are:

- debtor can appropriate any payment at time of payment;
- if debtor does not appropriate, creditor can;
- if neither appropriates, rule in *Clayton's* case applies.

In this case, the debtor has appropriated and, despite the unsatisfactory nature of the account, the bank has to comply (*Deeley* v *Lloyds* (1912)).

To stop this happening again, the bank should demand repayment of the borrowing unless the customer comes forward with satisfactory repayment proposals, as requested.

Part (b)

The implication is that, after one year, the executors will have ceased to act as executors and will now be operating as trustees and, as such, all must sign because, unlike executors, trustees cannot delegate authority amongst themselves.

However, transformation does not occur automatically after a certain time period – some estates take longer to wind up than others.

Activity on the account gives useful guidance – executors are involved in 'one-off' transactions, such as payment of funeral expenses – trustees will be making periodic, regular payments of income to beneficiaries.

If unsure, the bank would ask the executors and, depending on the reply, either continue account or convert to trust account with new mandate.

Part (c)

Section 349 Companies Act 1985 states that the company name needs to be clearly identified (on letters, bills of exchange, etc.).

The omission of the word 'Ltd' from the cheque book makes the directors personally liable to the holder of any cheque which is not paid (s.349).

Relevant cases on this point:

- *British Airways Board* v *Parish* (1979)
- *Maxform Spa* v *Mariani & Goodville Ltd* (1979).

In turn, directors might sue the bank for negligence in preparation of the cheques.

Fortunately, the account has good credit balances and cheques will be paid – therefore, no risk.

However, the bank will order new cheques, ask for the old cheque book to be returned, and apologise.

Comment

In all three parts a basic principle was involved which needed to be stated. The potential consequences of those principles then needed to be discussed and solutions provided.

May 1992 Q3

You have at your branch of Briggs Bank the account of Lohmann Ltd, and also that of A A Lilley, who works in the company's accounts department.

Today, you receive a visit from J Tyldesley, the finance director of the company. He tells you that over the past month Lilley has misappropriated company funds in the sum of £20,860 by:

(a) altering the amounts on cheques drawn in his favour in payment of expenses he had incurred;

(b) writing out cheques in his favour, and forging the signatures of the directors;

(c) paying into his own account cheques payable to various suppliers of the company – the cheques were all paid in at other branches of your bank;

(d) altering the payee's name on certain cheques payable to one particular supplier. These cheques were made out by

Lilley in favour of the supplier, A Alan, and, once they had been signed, he amended the name to A Alan Lilley and paid the cheques into his own account.

Mr Tyldesley argues that the bank had no authority to debit any of these cheques to the company's account, and requests repayment of the total sum involved.

Required:

Discuss the position of Briggs Bank in regard to each of the above claims, and state how you would respond to Mr Tyldesley's request. Give reasons for your answers.   (20)

Suggested answer

Part (a)

Were the alterations apparent or not? If apparent, and not confirmed by drawer's initial, then the bank has no defence and will have to refund the amount by which the cheques were increased.

If not apparent, have the alterations been facilitated by drawer's negligence in completing cheques, as in the case *London Joint Stock Bank* v *MacMillan & Arthur* (1918)?

The bank's liability will depend on the degree of the drawer's negligence; if any, customers have a duty of care in completing cheques (*Joachimson* v *Swiss Bank Corporation* (1921)).

Part (b)

A forged drawer's signature makes cheques totally inoperative (s.24 Bills of Exchange Act 1882).

The bank has no authority, therefore, to debit customer's account and will have to refund those amounts involved.

Part (c)

This situation is similar to the *Lloyds Bank* v *Savory* case (1933).

The bank has been negligent in collecting cheques (drawn by the employer in favour of suppliers) for the account of an employee without enquiry.

They have, therefore, lost the protection of s.4 Cheques Act 1957.

Paying in at another branch does not change the position – it is all one bank.

The bank will have to refund amounts involved.

Part (d)

This situation is similar to the case *Slingsby* v *District Bank Ltd* (1932), i.e. involving addition in the space after payee's name.

The decision on this case held that it was not negligent of a drawer to leave such a space and therefore liability fell on the paying bank.

It is no defence that the addition was non-apparent. Nevertheless, the cheque has been materially altered and the drawer is not liable (s.64 Bills of Exchange Act 1882).

The bank will have to refund the relevant amounts.

Comment

There was no need for technique in this question. Each part was purely factual requiring knowledge of case law and appropriate statute. A further point which could have been added to the answers, concerning all four parts, was that the bank would need to see the cheques in question before making any refunds. Also, the bank should have been suspicious of such amounts going through the customer's account.

May 1992 Q4

(a) During a current inspection of your branch, the account of Denis Smith, which is overdrawn by £4,652, is brought to your attention. Mr Smith is a wealthy individual, and you have always been prepared to allow his account to go overdrawn, without any formal agreement, in the knowledge that substantial dividend payments, which always restore the account to credit, are received each June and December. This arrangement has worked satisfactorily for a number of years, and the maximum overdraft on the account has never exceeded £7,000.

Today, the inspector mentions that, as the account has been permanently overdrawn since 3 February 1992, you are now legally obliged to formalise certain aspects of this arrangement with Mr Smith.

Required:

Explain the legal requirement which prompted the inspector's comment, and state what action you would take. Give reasons for your answer.

(6)

(b) Today, you receive a visit from William Storer. Mr Storer is a director of a family-owned business, Storer & Co Ltd, which banks at your branch, and he calls to advise you that the family has decided to place the company in liquidation. He also informs you that the necessary statutory declaration has been made by the directors, and that a formal meeting to wind up the company is being held next week.

The present balance on the company account is credit £2,580, and Mr Storer mentions that several cheques totalling £1,875 have been issued over the last few days. He would like these cheques to be paid on presentation.

Required:

(i) State briefly what type of liquidation this appears to be, and explain the meaning of, and rules relating to, 'the necessary statutory declaration'.   (6)

(ii) Explain what steps the bank should take and discuss the likely course of events, including any further action to be taken by the bank, in the event that a resolution to wind up the company is passed. Give reasons for your answer.
(8)

Suggested answer

Part (a)

This is based on the principle that overdrafts, without any formal agreement, which are still outstanding after three months, are subject to the Consumer Credit Act 1974.

It applies only to lending of £15,000, or less, to non-corporate customers.

A customer now has to be supplied with certain information (as under all CCA agreements), i.e. APR applicable, details of charges.

These rules in respect of overdrafts came into effect in February 1990.

Part (b)

(i) This type of winding up is a 'members' voluntary'.

The statutory declaration is the declaration of solvency made by the directors.

Section 89 Insolvency Act 1986, requires a declaration that the company will be able to pay its debts in full within 12 months of the commencement of the winding up.

The declaration has to be made in the five-week period prior to the passing of the resolution to wind up and must include a statement of assets and liabilities.

The declaration must be delivered to the registrar of companies within 15 days after resolution to wind up.

(ii) Directors' powers cease only when the resolution to wind up has been passed.

Therefore, the account can be continued normally — cheques can be paid within the credit balance.

The bank will note the date of the meeting and will want to know if the resolution to wind up was passed.

The bank will want to see a copy of the resolution winding up the company and appointing a liquidator.

The bank will also want confirmation that the declaration of solvency was filed correctly, otherwise members have no power to appoint a liquidator.

The bank will no longer accept instructions from directors.

The liquidator will be allowed to operate the existing account or a new one can be opened in the liquidator's name.

Comment

Again, not much examination technique was needed. The question embraced mostly technical matters although some procedural practice was called for, especially in the last part.

May 1992 Q5

(a) In each of the following situations, demand has been made by the bank on the guarantor, who denies liability. Each of the guarantees is on the bank's standard form, and none of the guarantors were customers of the bank at the time of signing the guarantee document. Discuss the bank's position, giving reasons for your answers.

(i)   Mr A says that, when he signed the guarantee, he was not aware that the principal debtor's husband, who was in fact an undischarged bankrupt, had power to sign on the principal debtor's account. He therefore claims the guarantee is invalid.   (4)

(ii)   Mr B says that, although the bank demanded repayment from him on 4 November 1991, in the sum of £1,500, the principal debtor's account was allowed to continue unbroken. Since the date of demand, sufficient credits have gone through the account to pay off the debt as it existed on that date. He therefore claims that he is no longer liable, and that he cannot be responsible for any indebtedness created by cheques paid since 4 November 1991.   (5)

(iii) Mr C says that, when he signed the guarantee, he was illiterate, and thus had no idea of the written terms of the form. He goes on to say that, before signing the guarantee, he had asked about its terms and had been told that it covered one specific advance. Had he known its terms made him liable for all borrowings of the principal debtor, he would not have signed the form. Accordingly he claims that the bank is unable to rely on the guarantee.   (6)

(b) Explain why a bank should no longer accept an equitable charge over unregistered land from a customer who merely wishes to deposit the title documents without completion of a form of charge.   (5)

Suggested answer

Part (a)

(i) *Cooper* v *National Provincial Bank Ltd* (1946) involved similar circumstances.

The decision in that case held that bank had no obligation to disclose information about the customer's account, and that the guarantee was good.

The decision based on the fact that guarantees are not contracts *uberrimae fides*.

The guarantor is still liable.

(ii) The guarantor is saying that the rule in *Clayton's* case has cleared the debt for which he is liable.

However, guarantee forms contain a clause which renders the guarantor still liable should the bank omit to stop the debtor's account.

The case *Westminster Bank* v *Cord* (1940) upheld the validity of this clause.

Therefore, the guarantor is still liable for the current debt.

(iii) The guarantor is claiming *'non est factum'*.

The circumstances are similar to *Lloyds Bank* v *Waterhouse* (1990).

Provided that the guarantor's illiteracy can be shown and that the guarantor did all he could to establish the nature and extent of his liability (e.g. asking suitable questions) and provided that the bank, by its conduct, caused him to believe he was signing something different to the actual document, the guarantor will be able to successfully claim '*non est factum*'.

The guarantor, therefore, will not be liable.

Part (b)

Previously, mere deposit created an equitable charge – *Harrold* v *Plenty* (1901).

However, s.2 Law of Property (Miscellaneous Provisions) Act 1989, requires contracts for the future disposition of an interest in land to be in writing, signed by all parties, and to include express terms agreed by the parties.

This means, that for an effective equitable charge, the bank will require a memorandum of deposit signed by both the customer and the bank.

Comment

This was a straightforward question which tested the knowledge of bank guarantee forms, which should be familiar from previous studies. Part (b) showed the importance of candidates keeping up to date with new legislation.

May 1992 Q6

Your customer, George Brann Ltd, is currently overdrawn £16,152 against a limit of £25,000. As security, you have an unlimited joint and several guarantee from the directors, George and Alex Hearne, and legal charges over separate life policies, taken out by the company, on each of their lives. Each policy is for £30,000 with a current surrender value of £9,640.

You have just been informed that Alex Hearne died yesterday.

Required:

(a) State what action, if any, you would take now to protect the bank's position, and explain the further steps you would need to put in hand over the next few weeks. (10)

(b) Explain how your answer would have differed, if at all, if the life policies had been taken out by the directors on their own lives, and charged to the bank in support of their guarantees. (10)

Suggested answer

Part (a)

No need to stop the company account because a company is entitled to proceeds of life policy and the bank is not concerned in preserving the deceased's liability under the guarantee.

The bank has only to collect proceeds of policy and credit to company accounts, i.e. £30,000.

The bank will need a copy of the death certificate to send to the insurance company, along with the policy and assignment (not re-assignment).

The bank will complete the insurance company's official receipt for the proceeds.

The bank will discuss the future conduct of the company with the surviving director, e.g. will another director need to be appointed? – presumably the limit can be cancelled and a guarantee placed on cancelled documents file.

Part (b)

In this situation, the company account will have to be stopped to preserve the liability of the deceased's estate for the company debt, i.e. to prevent the operation of *Clayton's* case (despite the protective clause in the guarantee form).

A new account will have to be opened for the company to be kept in credit, unless new borrowing arrangements are made.

The bank will collect the proceeds of the policy (as before) but this time credit the suspense account for the time being.

The bank could clear the company debt and give the surplus to the deceased's personal representatives, but the personal representatives would have a right of contribution from the surviving director under the joint and several guarantee.

Once a satisfactory agreement has been reached, the bank will release the surplus funds to the deceased's personal representatives, after seeing the probate or letters of administration.

Comment

This was a procedural question on action required on the death of the life assured. A few other principles were tested (e.g. the treatment of proceeds) but since a similar question was asked previously, there was no excuse for not scoring high marks.

May 1992 Q7

(a) You are the manager of a branch of Brown Bank, and have recently been successful in tendering for the account of McLaren Fry Ltd, a publishing company banking with one of your competitors. As part of the tender you agreed to provide borrowing facilities of £280,000 against the security of a debenture incorporating a fixed charge over the company's freehold premises and a floating charge over all other assets.

All the company's invoices are, and will continue to be, factored, and a reserve of 20% of the monthly debtor's figure is retained by the factoring company, which has a fixed charge over the book debts.

The freehold premises (unregistered land) were professionally valued on a forced sale basis at £250,000 in March 1992, and you have calculated the break-up value of the remaining assets, net of factored debts, at £75,000.

Required:

Set out, in note form, all the steps necessary for taking and perfecting this security.   (14)

(b) You have at your branch of Old Bank the account of Turnbull Ltd, a wholly-owned subsidiary of Wainwright plc.

Today, the directors of Turnbull Ltd approach you for a short-term overdraft facility of £150,000. They offer as security a letter of comfort from the parent company.

Required:

Discuss the enforceability of a letter of comfort as a form of security. You should support your answer by reference to case law.   (6)

Suggested answer

Part (a)

- Examine memorandum and articles of association for company and directors' power to borrow and charge security.

- Some banks no longer do this, relying on s.35 Companies Act 1985.

- Obtain professional valuation.

- Obtain title deeds – have report on title done.

- Usual searches – Companies House, Land Charges Registry, local authority.

- Obtain fire policy – give notice to insurance company (company property).

— Execute debenture form – both company and bank to sign (s.2 Law of Property (Miscellaneous Provisions) Act 1989).

– Bank will have to give priority to factoring company in respect of book debts, although any surplus funds from the reserve will be due to bank.

– Debenture to be registered within 21 days of execution at Companies House (s.395 Companies Act 1985) otherwise void against liquidator, administrator or any creditor.

– Wait 21 days after registration, then search Companies House again to ensure debenture has been registered and no other interests have been registered since the previous search.

Part (b)

Letters of comfort were always regarded as 'non security' because they were unenforceable.

It was stated, however, in the cases *Kleinwort Benson Ltd* v *Malaysian Mining Corporation Berhad* (1987) and *Chemco Leasing* v *Rediffusion Ltd* (1987) that enforceability depends on the intention of the parties.

Therefore, it depends on the wording of the documentation as to whether the parties intend to be legally bound, or not, by the terms of the letter of comfort.

Comment

This was another procedural question in part (a), whilst part (b) dealt with a matter which did cause confusion at the time of the cases but which is now well established.